have two main aims:
n using and reading
:ical vocabulary, to sup-
:he basic mathematical
concepts introduced to young children.

Bird has three eggs
Illustrated by Paul Price-Smith

Mathematical content
The story is used as a simple introduction to one-to-one correspondence.

Vocabulary content

Mathematical words
three some too many too few one

Words with picture clues
Bird eggs babies presents Bronto Frog tea

Other words
has for your says Oh don't cry have this thank you stop and

Nuffield Maths 5-11

General editor:
E.A. Albany

Longman

BRONTO
BOOKS
SET D

Bird has three eggs

Wendy Dewhirst

Bird has three eggs.

Bird has three babies.

“Here are some presents
for you three babies,”
says Bronto.

"Oh. Too many,"
says Bronto.

"Here are some presents for you three babies," says Frog.

"Oh. Too few,"
says Frog.

"Don't cry.
Have this one,"
says Frog.

"Thank you
Bronto and Frog.
Stop for tea."

Further activities

These suggestions are planned to extend the mathematical ideas that are found in this book, and to give additional practice in using and reading the vocabulary involved.

Chart showing eggs, babies, hats, scarves.

See Nuffield Maths 1 *Teacher's Handbook* for further activities involving matching one-to-one.

Giving out papers, pencils, etc., provides useful experience of one-to-one matching. Setting the table for a meal; one plate for each place, one knife, one fork, etc.

The *Puffin Book of Card Games* is a useful source for games involving dealing out, matching, memory.
Concept Snap is obtainable from Language Development Assoc., Park Works, Norwich Road, Wisbech.

Creative activities may include painted eggs, egg-shell mosaics, feather collage, painting of the story.

Story sequence activity:

1	2	3	4	5	6

The child draws six pictures of the story in sequence. Follow-up recording may result with adult help—this is a useful check for memory and language understanding.

Nuffield Maths 5-11

BRONTO
BOOKS
SET D

BRONTO BOOKS

Set A ISBN 0 582 18880 6	Counting with Bronto Counting backwards Comparing with Bronto Poor Bronto Up and down Round red apple
Set B ISBN 0 582 18881 4	Bronto joins the circus Action words Mini half-as-big Left, right Greedy pig Snail's walk
Set C ISBN 0 582 18882 2	Animal shapes My dad's garage Bronto time Words for things In and out 3 buses
Set D ISBN 0 582 18883 0	Bird, Frog and Bronto Bird has three eggs Bronto and the rocket Bronto at the zoo Bronto at the fair Bronto visits the dentist

LONGMAN GROUP LIMITED
Longman House, Burnt Mill, Harlow, Essex, U.K.

Published for the Nuffield Foundation
by Longman Group Limited 1979
Second impression 1981
ISBN 0 582 18883 0
Printed in Hong Kong by
Sheck Wah Tong Printing Press Ltd.

Longman